TEXTURES

OF HIS

QUILT

With photographs and prose by the author

Tim Tweedie

Dunecrest Press

The author gratefully acknowledges :
Judy Tweedie, the author's wife for
her patience, suggestions and proofing
of the photography and prose; the author's father,
Herbert C. Tweedie, for instilling in the
author his love for photography and
searching for the beauty in all of God's
creation; and the author's mother,
Marjorie Tweedie, for her encouragement
of all the author's creative endeavors.

Printed in the U.S.A. by Dunecrest Press, Long Beach, Washington

ISBN: 978-1-945539-30-5

CONTENTS

Forward

Page 8   His Invitation

Page 10   His Plan

Page 14   His Creation

Page 18   The Day Begins

Page 22   The Waters Awake

Page 26   The Sea

Page 30   Beneath The Sea

Page 34   Snow and Ice

Page 38   Rivers

Page 44   Lakes

Page 50   The Mountains

Page 54   The Sky

Page 58   Struggle and Grow

Page 64   The Attentive Gardener

Page 70   Abundance

Page 76   God's Gifts

Page 80   Paths

Page 84   Another Day Will Come

Location of Photos

FORWARD

This book is a product of my enjoyment of both photography and prose. It's mostly filled with what I hope are inspiring panoramas, especially of mountains, lakes, seas, and skies. But I've also focused in on smaller moments too. I'm looking primarily at nature's varying beauty throughout the day. Therefore, I've tried to take man-made items out of all but a few pictures. I prefer to speak through the voice and emotions evoked by nature. I try to seize the textures and composition of the variety in God's quilt with which he covers his earth. I pray I've succeeded.

My interest in photography and in writing prose has evolved over many years. Probably watching my father's love for the people and places he would capture with his camera, and then share them in the resulting "slide shows", led me to my first camera. Watching my father's excitement as he discovered a pristine mountain lake and angled for the best picture developed in me a sense of wonder and positioning for the many pictures around us each day.

I especially enjoyed panoramic scenes, anything that overpowered my senses and left me amazed and in wonder of God's creation.
Gradually I took the time to look everywhere, finding the fragile wildflower near the trail which may only live for a few days, or seeing the trickle of a small spring hugging the rocks on a bush shrouded mountainside, each becoming framed in six square feet of mystery and awe. All of these made my heart beat faster, and I believe, made me a better and more complete person for having experienced them. This is what I hope my pictures may do for others as they experience a never to be repeated moment in

time and feel this excitement and beauty deep
inside. I'm offering a chance to pause for a
moment in a hectic day, and for a few seconds
disappear into the picture, with the thought, "I
wish I were here". If the viewer can feel any of
these emotions when looking at my pictures, I'll
feel blessed.

My writing and enjoyment of poetry and prose
came later. One day while taking notes in class
after years of writing on task for various degrees,
I found as I wrote in the margins, that I liked to
write poetry. The more bored I became, the more
the margins filled, and the better I gradually
became at filling those margins. Then when I had a
chance to write for a card company which
preferred prose, I switched. Lo and behold, I
enjoyed prose too. So my writing grew from my
schooling and then evolved with my desire to
describe my surroundings and the various feelings
they produced.

I hope you'll take a moment to read the prose that
precedes and describes each section and then let
yourself become part of each picture.

His Invitation

Reach out and touch
the textures of my quilt.

Use your eyes, hands, and mind.
Become one with them,
or merely get acquainted.

See the beauty of my creation.
The waves of color that explode
with the morning sun.
Or watch the evening's shade
slowly drawn upon the day,
casting nature's shadow
across the sky.

Grasp hold of my handiwork.
Feel the life and spirit that
dwell within.

Discover the many wonders,
shapes and sizes of the
earth's adornment.

For some you'll gently
bend your knee to see.
Yet others will fill the sky
before you, from miles away.

Then look and feel and listen
with your mind.
For my creation is only fully
comprehended and endeared
when you allow it to enter
your heart.

His Plan

His shrouded creation
emerges from its shadowed roots.
His thoughts at first are clouded,
but then they are slowly shared.

It all fits together in his plan.
The sky, the sea, and the earth
which emerges from its salty foam.

It's old, yet it's new,
created over eons,
or just in a day.

God will have his way
and we will follow,
as he lovingly leads us
through his creation.

We're allowed a visit,
a ride upon its surface
for a determined number of years.

We see its beauty, taste its pleasures,
and feel the textures of the land and waters
beneath our feet.

God's quilt of many different shapes and colors.
His gift to us.

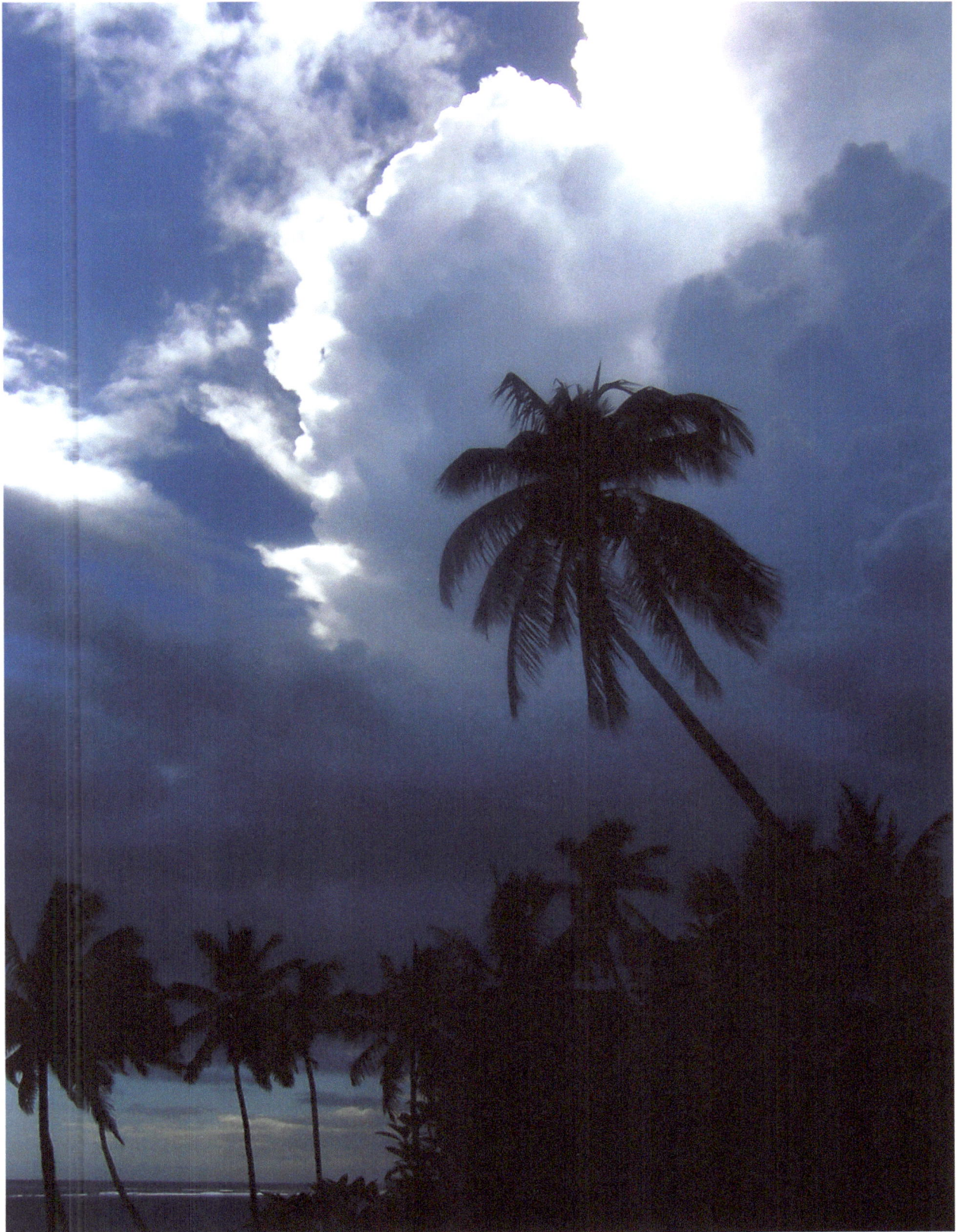

His Creation

From fire, heat, and smoke,
his earth will awaken.

From darkness, light blesses its surface.
Water and earth can now
emerge from his firmament.

God breathes and life begins,
preparing the way
for what may be an eternity
of sunrises and sunsets
over an ever changing planet.

He has spoken,
and we will see and hear,
and obey.

The Day Begins

The mystery remains for a time.

The light begins to set the mountains aglow.
Yet, the darkness refuses to release its grip
while fighting to keep at least a portion
under its control.

The cloud's sympathies lie with darkness,
but it realizes it must let the mountains through
to join the morning sky.

The sea too demands attention,
along with its adjoining land.

The clouds and the darkness
know they'll have another day.

The Waters Awake

The waters begin to rise,
creeping higher upon the sand,
and pounding harder
against the rocky shores.

They work hard to shape the land,
and find a companion
in the wind and the rain.

They crash, then whisper,
in the same chord.

They will do their duty,
as God has carefully instructed.

Nature knows its seasons,
each with its own character
and personality,
each contributing according
to its time.

The Sea

The sea reflects its many faces
upon the shore and sky.

The earth's dark veil slowly lifts.
First light appears
written upon the morning clouds.

It calls to you,
to travel upon its endless waters.
Explore with me,
let's search out distant shores
which only a few have seen.
Glide upon my waves to see the marvels
that I have done, in his name.

Yet beware, for I do have a temper.
I will rise and fall and roar
with my friend the wind.
I will break you upon the rocks,
if you are careless.

But I will also cradle you,
in my arms, at the end of the day.
I will gently rock you asleep,
in the breathless beauty of his creation.

Beneath the Sea

I hold beneath my waves a world so immense
that only God knows its true depth and scope.
Marvels so vast and life so splendid
that just a peek into my bosom
will excite your soul and ignite your passions.

My tenants that dwell within
are numbered by their creator.
He knows each one,
as he knows and loves all of us.

Each life form holds its own secrets
waiting to be explored.
waiting to be discovered.

Immerse yourself into the sea.
Be one with me, if only for a moment.

Snow and Ice

The snow and ice are the hand tools of God.
They are the first to start his miracle
of sculpture and wear.

On the heights of his earth the snow falls,
becoming the water that feeds the lakes and rivers,
becoming the ice that lays bare
the very crust of the earth.

Pushing, grinding, expanding, cracking,
devouring mountains that stand in its way.
Creating valleys so sharp and deep
that even the sun's light can't find their depth,
but only for a moment each day.

The ice too knows its task
and does it well.
Looking back,
as its mighty powers melt away,
to view its amazing handiwork,
To see what artists only dream of copying.

Rivers

God also placed water upon the land.

His rain and snow created
the brothers to the sea,
the lakes and rivers.

They too have a task as textures
in his plan.
For they must carve and shape the land,
and form the mountains,
valleys, and canyons of his world.

Rock and earth give way to the power
of his rivers and falls.
Their voices are often heard for miles,
endlessly telling tales of their journey,
while displaying their cascading mane
of white for all to see.

Yet their boasting soon mellows
as the land begins to yield
to the river's changing mood.

It now sings in soft tones,
splashing and moaning,
as it meanders over
land and meadow.

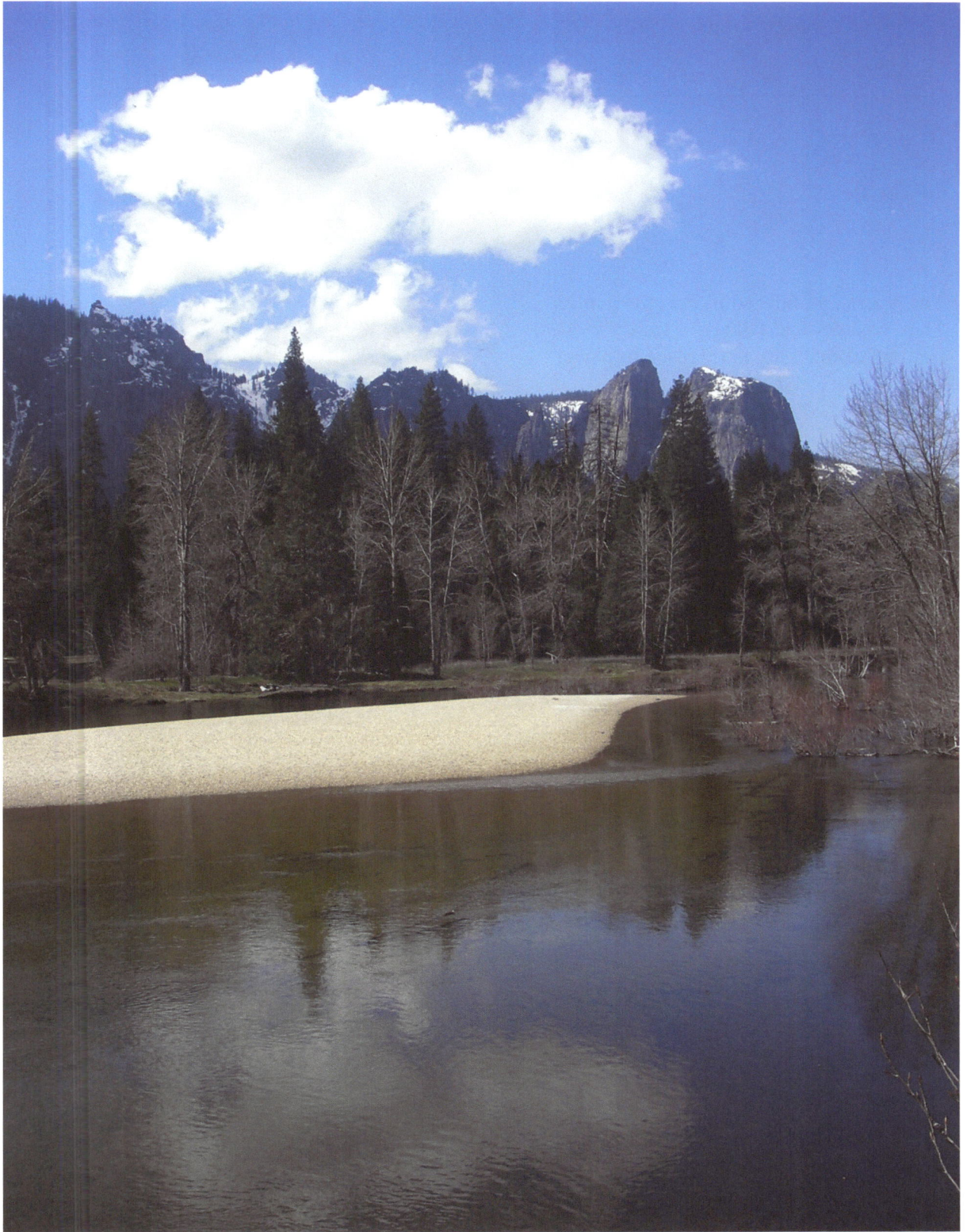

Lakes

The rivers and falls soon become gentle.
They whisper and take their time,
running effortlessly from place to place.
They explore and search for a new
place to rest, if only for a moment.

They grace, like a gem,
the mountains that entrap them.
They display their admiration
for their friends nearby,
through reflections upon
their mirrored faces.

Tranquil and calm lakes allow nature
a chance to adorn their surroundings
with wreathes of different foliage and colors.
One for each season and phase
of their lives.

The Mountains

The mountains stand as sentinels
above the earth.
Though battered and beaten
by the ice and the snow,
their grandeur is not diminished.

Instead, their profiles are cut and polished,
their features enhanced.
The lines and cracks
of age and wisdom appear,
slowly changing their grand silhouette
against the sky.

They reach up
and gather the clouds around them.
A robe of gray and white
to amuse his highness.

But as the snow falls anew
covering their vanity,
they are again reminded
of the power of their maker,
and their assigned task
in nature's quilt.